NATIVE AMERICAN LEGENDS
TECUMSEH

Don McLeese

Rourke
Publishing LLC
Vero Beach, Florida 32964

www.rourkepublishing.com

PHOTO CREDITS:
©Library of Congress: Title, pgs 5, 18, 21, 22, 25, 27
©Hulton/Archive by Getty Images: pgs 9, 11
©Canadian Heritage, National Archives of Canada: Cover, pgs 6, 13
©James P. Rowan: pg 17
©PhotoDisc, Inc: pg 14

Title page: *A painting of the Battle of the Thames and the death of Tecumseh in 1813*

Editor: Frank Sloan

Cover and page design by Nicola Stratford

Library of Congress Cataloging-in-Publication Data

McLeese, Don.
  Tecumseh / Don McLeese.
    p. cm. -- (Native American legends)
Summary: A brief biography of the famous leader of the Shawnee who tried to get other tribes to join him in opposing the Europeans who wanted to take their land.
Includes bibliographical references and index.
  ISBN 1-58952-731-3 (hardcover)
  1. Tecumseh, Shawnee chief, 1768-1813--Juvenile literature. 2. Shawnee Indians--Kings and rulers--Biography--Juvenile literature. 3. Shawnee Indians--Government relations--Juvenile literature. [1. Tecumseh, Shawnee chief, 1768-1813. 2. Shawnee Indians--Biography. 3. Indians of North America--East (U.S.)--Biography. 4. Kings, queens, rulers, etc.] I. Title. II. Series.
  E99.S35T166 2003
  974.004'973--dc21

2003005100

Printed in the USA

w/w

Table of Contents

The Shawnee Chief 4

Tecumseh's Childhood 8

The Prophet 10

A Miracle? 12

Prophetstown 16

The Battle of Tippecanoe 20

Tecumseh's Return .24

Death of a Great Warrior 26

Tecumseh's People .28

Time Line 29

Glossary 30

Further Reading/Website to Visit 31

Index 32

Tecumseh was a great **chief** of the **Shawnee tribe** of **Native Americans**. In English, his name means "Shooting Star." During the early 1800s, he tried to get other tribes to join together with the Shawnees to keep white settlers from taking their land. Native Americans believed that no one can own the land, and that it belongs to everyone.

When white people came to America from Europe, they moved to land where Native Americans had been living for centuries. The settlers called this land **frontier** or "wilderness." After they found Native Americans living there, the white leaders tried to buy the land from the tribes or fight them for it.

A Currier and Ives print gives an idea of American frontier life in the 1800s.

Tecumseh knew that no one tribe was strong enough to keep the land from the white settlers. But if all the tribes came together, perhaps they could continue to live on the land they loved. Tecumseh wanted all the tribes to promise that they wouldn't sell land to the new settlers. If the white men tried to take the land from them, they would fight for it.

Tecumseh was a strong leader, a powerful speaker, and a very brave man. Even after his tribe lost its land in battles with white soldiers, the Native Americans never lost respect for their chief.

"Shooting Star"
Many Native Americans were given names from things they could see in nature. A "shooting star" is another name for a meteor, which moves brightly and quickly across the night sky.

◄ *A print of Tecumseh by Frederick H. Brigden*

Tecumseh was born in 1768. His tribe lived in Ohio, and his father was the chief. Tecumseh had five brothers and one sister.

When Tecumseh was only six years old, his father was killed by white settlers. Tecumseh's oldest brother taught him how to become a Shawnee **warrior**. Tecumseh wanted to be just like his father.

Tecumseh was 15 when he fought in his first real battle. His tribe took one white man as a **prisoner** and burned him. Tecumseh thought this was bad, and he said he would never treat a prisoner that way.

Tecumseh was always a leader. The enemy he and his ➤
friends pretended to fight as children was the white man.

Tecumseh's Family

His father, Puckeshinwau, was also a very great chief. His mother, Methoatske, was one of the smartest members of the tribe. Chiksika, the older brother who taught Tecumseh, was one of the tribe's best with a bow and arrow.

The Prophet

Tecumseh's youngest brother was named Lalawethika (sometimes spelled "Lalawathika" or "Laulewasika"). In English, his name means "Noise Maker." He was always bragging loudly to other people, and he was jealous of his older brother, Tecumseh. Lalawethika was born in 1775.

When he grew older, he drank a lot of alcohol, which made him act foolish. One night in 1805, he had a **vision**, which he said was sent by the Great Spirit. Lalawethika said the vision had changed him. He had become a holy man and he would no longer drink alcohol.

In 1805 Lalawethika changed his name to Tenskwatawa, meaning "Open Door" (or "I am the door"). Others called him "the **Prophet**," which means a holy man who can see into the future. Many Native Americans came to believe that the Prophet had special powers.

The Great Spirit
In Native American religions, the Great Spirit was their version of God. The Great Spirit would send visions to some of them that other Native Americans couldn't see.

Tenskwatawa was Tecumseh's brother. He was shot in the eye with an arrow by accident and lost the sight of that eye.

A Miracle?

General William Henry Harrison was governor of the Indiana Territory where the Shawnees and other tribes lived. He wanted that land for the white settlers of the United States. He worried that if too many Native Americans followed Tecumseh and the Prophet that they would keep their land.

He said that if the Prophet was really a holy man, he should be able to make a miracle happen. He said the Prophet should make the sun stand still. If he couldn't, thought Harrison, no one should believe that the Prophet had special powers.

The Prophet and his brother, the Shawnee war chief Tecumseh

The Prophet knew something that the governor didn't. There would be an **eclipse** on June 16, 1806. During an eclipse of the sun, the moon moves between the earth and the sun, and the sky turns black. Just before noon of that day, the Prophet pointed to the sky and asked the Great Spirit to make the sun black.

Everything turned dark, as if day had become night. Native Americans thought that the Prophet had caused this by asking the Great Spirit. Even more Native Americans started believing that the Prophet was a holy man who they should follow.

When the moon passes between the earth and the sun, a solar eclipse occurs.

In 1808, Tecumseh and the Prophet moved their tribe west from Ohio to land where the Kickapoo and Potawatomi tribes were living. They all made a new village called "Prophetstown" in the Indiana Territory, beside the **Tippecanoe** River. They invited members of other tribes to join them.

Prophetstown became the capital for Native Americans, just as Washington, D.C. was the capital of the United States. It was a great area for hunting and fishing, so the tribes had lots of food. Tecumseh traveled to other tribes, asking them to join together to keep white settlers from taking their land.

A modern photograph of the Tippecanoe Battlefield Monument ➤

"No tribe has the right to sell the land," Tecumseh said. "Sell a country? Why not sell the air, the great sea, as well as the earth? Didn't the Great Spirit make them all for the use of his children?" Many Native Americans agreed with Tecumseh that the land was for sharing, not owning.

Indiana
The white settlers called the Native Americans "Indians," because early explorers thought they'd landed in India when they first came to America. Indiana didn't become one of the United States until 1816. Prophetstown was near what is now Lafayette, Indiana.

◄ *A hand-colored print of Tecumseh in full dress*

The Battle of Tippecanoe

As governor of the Indiana Territory, General Harrison wanted this land for the United States. Tecumseh knew this, so he traveled to the South to get more Native Americans to come to Prophetstown. He told the Prophet not to fight the white settlers until Tecumseh came back with more warriors.

A print showing William Henry Harrison at the Battle of Tippecanoe

The Prophet had fewer than 500 warriors, and General Harrison had almost 1,000 soldiers. But the Prophet believed that the Great Spirit wouldn't let him lose, so he ordered his men to attack the U.S. soldiers on November 7, 1811. The soldiers killed many of the warriors and burned Prophetstown to the ground.

President Harrison
After winning the battle against Tecumseh, William Henry Harrison was nicknamed "Tippecanoe."

◄ *William Henry Harrison became president of the United States in 1840 and died a year later in the White House.*

Tecumseh's Return

Tecumseh came back to Prophetstown three months later. He was very sad to see his town burned, and he was very angry at his brother. Because the Native Americans lost the battle, they no longer believed that the Prophet had any special powers. Tecumseh knew that Native Americans needed to stay together, but it was harder for him to convince others to share his dream.

In 1812, the United States declared war with
Great Britain over the freedom of ships.

When Great Britain and the United States started fighting the War of 1812, Tecumseh joined the British side. He thought that if the United States lost, the Native Americans would be able to keep their land.

The War of 1812
The British navy was very powerful and kept some American ships from going where they'd been sent. When the war was over, both sides said they had won.

Death of a Great Warrior

Many Native Americans joined Tecumseh, who showed the British that he was a great leader. After Tecumseh helped the British capture Detroit from the United States, he was killed in battle by General Harrison's army on October 5, 1813.

The dream of all Native Americans becoming one nation together died with Tecumseh. Though the United States took the land that had belonged to the Shawnees, Tecumseh was remembered as a hero.

Tecumseh was 45 when he was killed during a battle. ➤
This Currier and Ives print is hand colored.

"He was truly great," wrote an Indiana newspaper in 1820, "as a statesman, a warrior and a patriot."

The Battle of Detroit
What is now the city of Detroit was captured by the British in the War of 1812, though the United States soon took it back.

Tecumseh was the chief of a large tribe known as the Shawnee. Although they originated in what is now Ohio, they traveled as far as South Carolina and Tennessee.

After the Battle of Tippecanoe, the Shawnee moved to Missouri, Kansas, and Oklahoma. Today there are about 2,250 Shawnee living on reservations in Oklahoma.

Time Line

1768	Tecumseh is born.
1775	Tecumseh's younger brother, Lalawethika ("The Prophet"), is born.
1806	The Prophet predicts an eclipse.
1808	Tecumseh and the Prophet move their tribe to Prophetstown.
1811	U.S. soldiers burn Prophetstown to the ground.
1812	Tecumseh joins the British side against the United States in the War of 1812.
1813	Tecumseh dies in battle.
1816	Indiana becomes a state.

chief (CHEEF) — leader, head of a Native American tribe

eclipse (ee CLIPS) — when a star or moon moves in front of another and hides its light

frontier (frun TEER) — a wilderness that has yet to be settled

Native Americans (NAY tiv uh MARE ih cans) — those who lived in the land that is now the United States before explorers from Europe came

prisoner (PRIZZ nur) — someone captured by the enemy or put into prison

prophet (PRAH fet) — someone who gets messages from God and can see into the future

Shawnee (shaw NEE) — a tribe of Native Americans who lived in what is now Ohio and Indiana

Tecumseh (teh KUM suh) — a great Shawnee chief

Tippecanoe (TIP ee cuhn OOOH) — a river in what is now Indiana. Also the name of the battle fought near that river

tribe (TRYB) — one of the bands or nations of Native Americans

vision (VIH zhuhn) — something seen in a dream or a trance

warrior (WAHR ee ur) — a great fighter in battle

Further Reading

Fitterer, C. Ann. *Tecumseh: Chief of the Shawnee.*
Child's World, 2002

Gregson, Susan R. *Tecumseh: Shawnee Leader.*
Bridgestone Books. 2003

Koestler-Grack, Rachel A. *Tecumseh, 1768-1813.*
Bridgestone Books. 2003

Website to Visit

www.heidelberg.edu/FallenTimbers/FTbio-Tecumseh.html

Index

birth 8

death 26

eclipse 15

Great Spirit 11

Harrison, General William Henry 12, 20, 23

"Prophet, The" 10

Prophetstown 16

Shawnee tribe 4, 28

Tippecanoe 20

War of 1812 25

About The Author

Don McLeese is an award-winning journalist whose work has appeared in many newspapers and magazines. He earned his M.A. degree in English from the University of Chicago, taught feature writing at the University of Texas and has frequently contributed to the World Book Encyclopedia. He lives with his wife and two daughters in West Des Moines, Iowa.